Ky's Magical ADVENTURES
WHERE THE GARBAGE GOES

SIAN CUFFY-YOUNG
ILLUSTRATED BY DANIEL AIERS

Published December 6 2020

ISBN: 978-1-7362171-0-8

DISCLAIMER

Shelley-Ann Edwards - Barran, Werd Coach Limited

Proofreading by: Dixie-Ann Belle, BelleWorks Limited

Illustration by: Daniel Aiers

Book layout by: Reanelle Allen, Legacy Graphic Studio

Author photo courtesy of Kerlon Orr

Author clothing and styling courtesy

Ky was in class. She looked up at the clock and saw that it was almost break time. This made her think of her favourite snack.

Ping-a-ling-a-ling the bell rang, and off to the cafeteria she went.

"One fruit pack, please?" she asked politely.

"Here you go, sweetheart. Enjoy!" the shopkeeper responded.

Ky was excited! She quickly opened the wrapper and took out one of the delicious fruit gummies. One after the other, she popped the treats into her mouth until the pack was empty.

Soon her snack was finished, and all she had in her hand was the wrapper. The gummies were awesome while they lasted, so she didn't mind. Now it was time to throw the wrapper in the bin. But just as she dropped the wrapper into the bin, a sudden gust of wind blew and whipped the wrapper out of the bin and on to the ground.

PLASTIC

GARBAGE

"Oh no!" Ky exclaimed. "I have to put it back in the bin!"

You see, Ky was very careful not to litter. She ran after the wrapper as it went bouncing along the ground and tried to catch it. But every time she thought she had it, the wrapper slipped from her fingers and blew away. This was a very strange wind.

Then the wrapper went over the wall, out of the school and on to the pavement outside. Ky couldn't believe her eyes. She looked around quickly to find something to reach it. Then she saw a long stick. This would help her get the wrapper back!

Ky picked up the stick and tried to reach the wrapper. She tried to pull the wrapper back through the fence, so she could put it in the bin. She tried and tried and tried, but it just didn't budge.

"What am I going to do?" she thought.

Just as Ky was thinking of getting a longer stick, the school bell rang. Break had ended, and now she had to return to class. Ky was heartbroken. She had to leave the wrapper on the ground. She remembered what her mommy had told her about putting garbage into a bin. But this wasn't her fault. She really had tried to get the wrapper.

At home time when her mother came to pick her up, Ky was very sad. She sat on a chair just outside her classroom with her head hung low. Mommy noticed that Ky was not her usual happy self.

"What's wrong, Ky?" Mommy asked. "You look a little sad today. Is everything okay?"

Ky wasn't sure how to explain what had happened to her mother, but she knew she had to tell the truth.

"Mommy, after I ate my snack today, the wind blew the wrapper out of the garbage, and I tried everything to get it back, but I couldn't reach it!" Ky was almost in tears. "I'm so sorry, Mommy. Please don't be mad at me."

Ky stopped walking and looked down at her shoes. She couldn't look her mother in the face. But Mommy knew Ky had tried her best, so she stooped down and gently turned Ky's face toward hers.

"It's okay, Ky. Don't be so sad," her mother explained. "I know you tried your best, and that's all I ask of you. I am glad that you tried to get it."

"But Mommy, what's going to happen to it now?" asked Ky. She really wasn't sure what happened to the things people threw away.

"Well, let's hope it gets to the right place!" Mommy said, standing up and taking Ky by the hand.

Ky didn't feel so sad anymore, but she kept thinking about what Mommy had said. At home, Ky changed her clothes and had a bath. After dinner, she brushed her teeth and climbed into bed. When Mommy came to tuck her in, Ky was still thinking about the wrapper and where all the garbage went after people threw it into bins.

Ky listened to her bedtime story and said her prayers before Mommy kissed her goodnight.

"I really hope the wrapper got to the bin somehow, Mommy," Ky said quietly as she snuggled under her blanket.

"I hope so too," Mommy said and turned off the light, closing the door quietly behind her.

When Ky fell asleep, she began to dream about what happened that day. Then she heard a voice say, "Hello!" Suddenly, she was in the playground at school, but no one else was around. The only thing she saw was the wrapper. The wrapper was talking to her!

"Hi, I'm Wendy! Nice to meet you," the wrapper said. Ky was surprised, but she wasn't afraid.

"Hi, Wendy," Ky said. "I'm sorry I couldn't pick you up and put you back into the bin today."

"That's okay, Ky. I'm here to tell you that you put me in the right place. It was the wind that blew me on to the ground. I know you tried your best."

Then Ky thought for a moment. She still didn't know where the garbage went after going into the bin. Maybe she could ask Wendy.

"Wendy, do you know where garbage goes after we throw it into the bin?" Ky asked.

"Of course I do," Wendy replied. "Want to go for a ride? I can show you!"

Ky got excited. "Yes, I'd love that!"

"Then hop aboard! I have a few friends I want you to meet."

Ky looked around. She was a bit confused because she didn't see anything to hop on to.

Then in the blink of an eye, Wendy transformed into a beautiful magic carpet with fancy, gold edges and bright, beautiful colours like pink, yellow, orange, and green.

Ky hopped on to Wendy, and away they went! They swished and swayed high over buildings and dipped through the trees. Ky was enjoying the ride when Wendy dipped again and stopped.

"Here is our first stop, Ky," Wendy said. "Let's go meet Mellie the Mango."

"Where are we, Wendy?" Ky asked.

Before Wendy could answer, Mellie jumped in with a singing voice and said, "Well, hello there, Ky. You are at my home. Fruits and vegetables and leaves and branches come here to be made into something called compost."

"Compost?" That word was strange to Ky. "What's that?"

"Compost is what you make when you put all the leftover peels and skins from your kitchen together with things like grass and leaves from your yard. When you leave it to mix for a while, it changes into something that can help your plants grow strong and healthy."

"Wow!" Ky said. "That sounds hard to do."

"No, it isn't really hard, but you have to ask your mommy and daddy to help you," Mellie said.

"Time to go Ky," Wendy whispered.

"Oh, okay. Nice to meet you, Mellie," Ky said as she waved goodbye.

COMPOST HERE

Ky hopped aboard Wendy, and off they went again. They swished and swayed and dipped through trees until they landed at their second stop.

"Hi JJ, this is my new friend, Ky," Wendy said. "She wants to know what happens to garbage after people throw it in the bin."

"Hi Ky, I'm JJ," came the soft reply. JJ wasn't as loud and friendly as Mellie. He looked thoughtful and serious.

"Do you drink juice from a box sometimes?" he asked Ky.

"Yes, I do," Ky replied with a smile. "I love apple juice."

"Well, I'm a juice box like your apple juice box. We're called Tetra Paks," JJ explained. "When you're done with us, we end up here at a recovery factory where we get washed and made into new boxes."

"Ohhhhh." Ky wanted to know more. "Is that what you call recycling?"

"Yes! That's exactly what it is." JJ was happy that Ky knew about recycling.

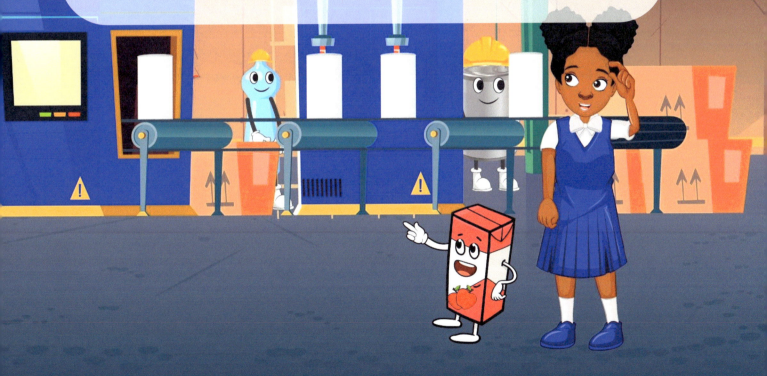

"We have one more stop to go, Ky!" Wendy interrupted.

"Thank you for the information, JJ. And it's nice to meet you." Ky waved goodbye to JJ, and off she and Wendy went.

They swished and swayed and dipped through the trees and finally landed at their third stop. But this place was nothing like what Ky had seen before.

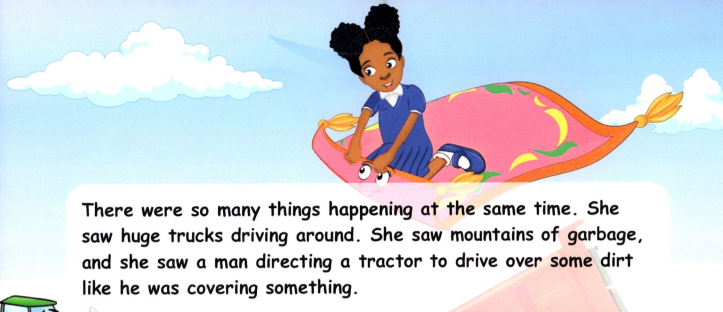

There were so many things happening at the same time. She saw huge trucks driving around. She saw mountains of garbage, and she saw a man directing a tractor to drive over some dirt like he was covering something.

"Hi Smelly, this is my new friend, Ky," Wendy said as she introduced Ky to Smelly the Garbage Truck.

"Hi Ky, nice to meet you," came a deep, deep voice. "This is where I come after I pick up your garbage from your house and school. This is called a landfill."

"A landfill?" Ky had never heard that word before. "But this place looks like a dump, and it smells funny too!"

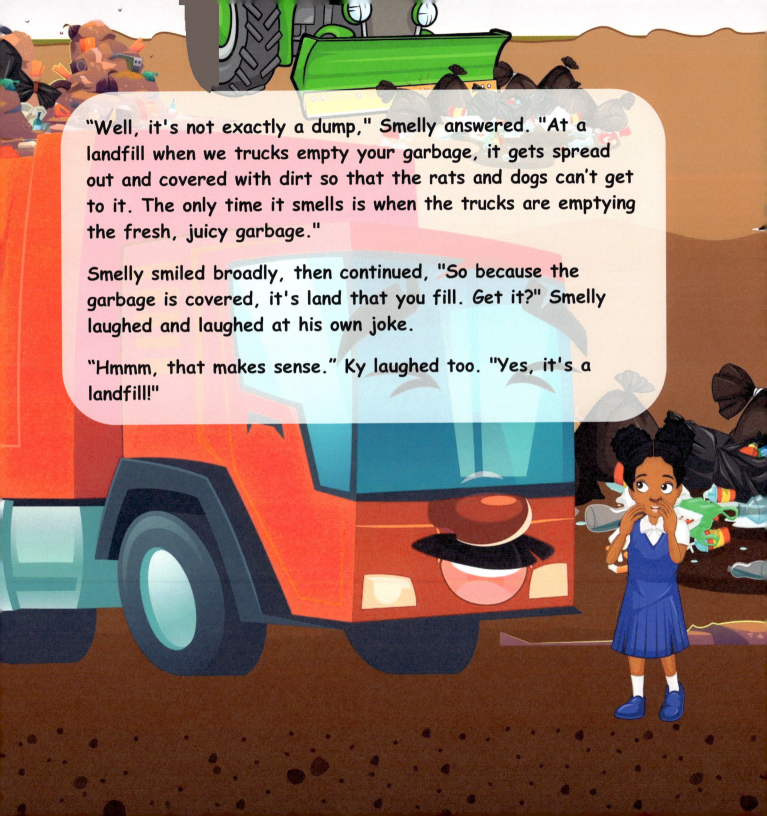

"Well, it's not exactly a dump," Smelly answered. "At a landfill when we trucks empty your garbage, it gets spread out and covered with dirt so that the rats and dogs can't get to it. The only time it smells is when the trucks are emptying the fresh, juicy garbage."

Smelly smiled broadly, then continued, "So because the garbage is covered, it's land that you fill. Get it?" Smelly laughed and laughed at his own joke.

"Hmmm, that makes sense." Ky laughed too. "Yes, it's a landfill!"

Ky looked around and noticed a few large, black birds flying around. She remembered seeing them before. She pointed to the birds and asked Smelly if he knew what they were called.

"Those birds? They are vultures. Here we call them corbeaux. They eat dead animals," Smelly explained.

"Ewwww!" Ky twisted up her nose as if she was smelling something terrible. "That sounds nasty!"

"Yup, you wouldn't want those birds to land on you," Smelly said and laughed his deep, rumbling laugh again, "but do you understand what we do here at the landfill?"

"Yes I do," Ky answered. "Thank you for showing me where the garbage goes!"

"You're welcome, Ky," Smelly replied. "Just keep putting all your garbage in the bin for me to collect!"

Just as Ky was answering Smelly, Wendy called, "Ky, it's time to go!"

"Bye, Smelly," Ky shouted as she hopped aboard Wendy. "It was nice meeting you!"

And off Wendy and Ky went, back to where they came from. Ky laughed as they went swishing and swaying and dipping through trees, high above the buildings until Ky was home again.

"Thanks, Wendy!" Ky said as she stepped off the magic carpet. "I am glad you took me to those places to meet your friends. I always wanted to know what happened to garbage after I threw it into the bin."

"Now you can tell all your friends at school," Wendy replied, "and remind them to always put their garbage into a bin."

"I sure will," Ky said excitedly.

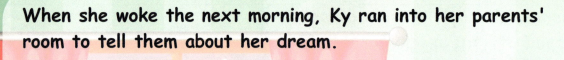

When she woke the next morning, Ky ran into her parents' room to tell them about her dream.

"Mommy, Daddy, you will never guess what I dreamt! I saw the wrapper I had yesterday, but then it wasn't a wrapper anymore. It spoke to me, and it turned into a magic carpet, and she took me on a ride!"

Ky was talking so fast that her parents could barely understand what she was saying. "Slow down, Ky," Mommy said with a laugh. She pulled Ky toward her in a hug. "Tell me what else happened?"

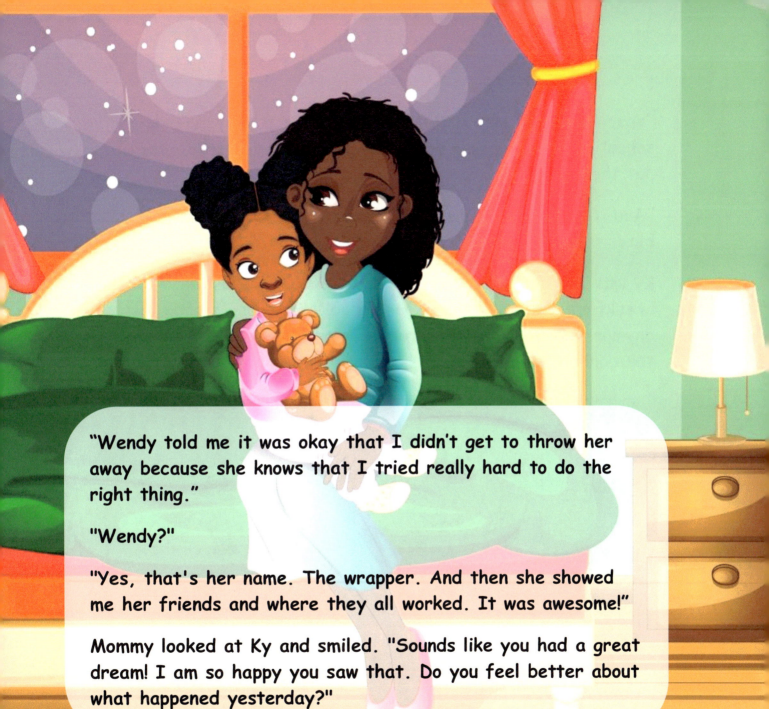

"Wendy told me it was okay that I didn't get to throw her away because she knows that I tried really hard to do the right thing."

"Wendy?"

"Yes, that's her name. The wrapper. And then she showed me her friends and where they all worked. It was awesome!"

Mommy looked at Ky and smiled. "Sounds like you had a great dream! I am so happy you saw that. Do you feel better about what happened yesterday?"

"Yes, Mommy, I do. And I cannot wait to tell my friends at school all about what I dreamt and to remind them to always put their garbage in a bin."

"And if it falls out, they should pick it up before the wind blows it away," Mommy added, and they both laughed.

Ky was so happy that she hummed a little tune as she had breakfast and got dressed for school. She wasn't sad anymore about losing the wrapper, and now she knew where the garbage went.

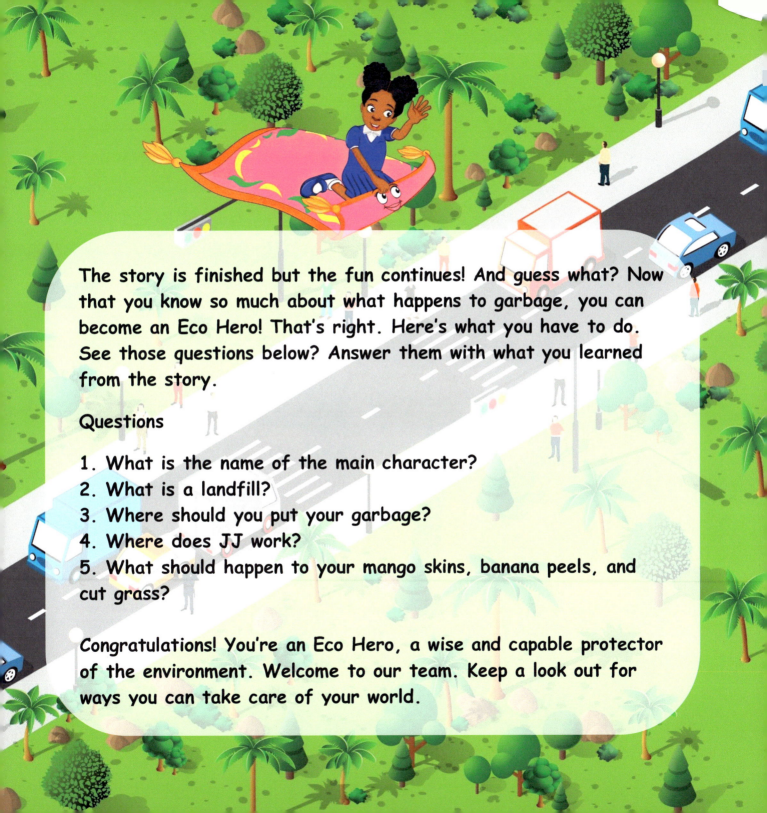

The story is finished but the fun continues! And guess what? Now that you know so much about what happens to garbage, you can become an Eco Hero! That's right. Here's what you have to do. See those questions below? Answer them with what you learned from the story.

Questions

1. What is the name of the main character?
2. What is a landfill?
3. Where should you put your garbage?
4. Where does JJ work?
5. What should happen to your mango skins, banana peels, and cut grass?

Congratulations! You're an Eco Hero, a wise and capable protector of the environment. Welcome to our team. Keep a look out for ways you can take care of your world.

I AM AN eco HeRO!

Made in the USA
Columbia, SC
12 September 2024

42200644R00022